# GUSTAV MAHLER

# *Symphonies Nos. 1 and 2*

## IN FULL SCORE

*Dover Publications, Inc., New York*

This Dover edition, first published in 1987, is a republication of the editions published by Josef Weinberger, Vienna, as *Erste Symphonie in D Dur* (n.d.) and *Zweite Symphonie in C Moll*. Below the Weinberger imprint on both title pages are the notices "in die Universal Edition aufgenommen" ["absorbed by Universal Edition"] and "für Deutschland bei Friedrich Hofmeister, Leipzig"; on the first page of the score of Symphony No. 2 appears the notice "Copyright 1897 by Friedrich Hofmeister, Leipzig." The list of instruments for Symphony No. 2 in the original German has been deleted; a table of contents, lists of instruments in English for both symphonies, and new English translations of the vocal texts of Symphony No. 2 have been added.

Manufactured in the United States of America
Dover Publications, Inc., 31 East 2nd Street, Mineola, N.Y. 11501

*Library of Congress Cataloging-in-Publication Data*

Mahler, Gustav, 1860–1911.
[Symphonies, no. 1, D major]
Symphonies nos. 1 and 2.

With alto solo in the 4th movement and solo voices (SA)
and chorus (SATB) in the 5th (2nd work).
Words of the 4th movement from Des Knaben Wunderhorn (Urlicht),
of the 5th by Klopstock (Auferstehung,
with additional verses by the composer) (2nd work).
Originally published: Vienna : J. Weinberger.
1. Symphonies—Scores.   I. Mahler, Gustav, 1860–1911.
Symphonies, no. 2, C minor. 1987.
M1001.M21 no. 1   1987      87-751545
ISBN 0-486-25473-9 (pbk.)

# Contents

# Note

This volume reprints the original published versions of both symphonies. A revised version of Symphony No. 1 was published by Universal Edition in 1906. That version contains hardly a single change in the first three movements; in the last movement a few measures were reorchestrated, some footnotes were added, and a handful of other minor changes were made. Symphony No. 2 appeared in two revised editions before Mahler's death; the revisions are more extensive than in Symphony No. 1. The changes are primarily in the orchestration; the final version contains precisely the same number of measures as the original, and the basic musical content of each measure is unchanged.

# SYMPHONY NO. 1

# *List of Instruments*

4 Flutes [Flöte, Fl.], two alternating on
    2 Piccolos [Piccolo, Picc.]
4 Oboes [Oboe, Ob.], one alternating on
    English Horn [Engl. Horn]
4 Clarinets [Clarinette, Clar.] (B♭, C, E♭, A), one alternating on
    Bass Clarinet [Bass-Clarinette, Basscl.] (B♭)—"doubled at least"
      in last movement
3 Bassoons [Fagott, Fag.], one alternating on
    Contrabassoon [Contra-Fagott, Contrafag.]

7 Horns [Horn] (F), with "reinforcement" in last movement
4 Trumpets [Trompete, Trmp.] (F, B♭), with added Trumpet in last
      movement
3 Trombones [Posaune, Pos.]
Tuba [Tuba]

4 Timpani [Pauken] (2 players)
Cymbals [Becken]
Triangle [Triangel]
Tam-tam [Tam-Tam]
Bass Drum [Grosse Trommel, Gr. Tr.]

Harp [Harfe]

Violins [Violine, Viol.] I, II
Violas [Viola]
Cellos [Violoncello, Cello]
Basses [Contrabass, Bass]

# Symphony No. 1

## 1

Anmerkung für den Dirigenten: Dieses tiefste a muss sehr deutlich wenngleich pp gespielt werden.

*) Wenn der Tubist diesen tiefen Ton nicht *pp* herausbringt, so ist derselbe dem Contrafagott zuzutheilen.

**19**

**19**

24   *SYMPHONY NO. 1 IN D MAJOR*

Von hier ab wird das Tempo bis zum Zeichen ⊕ in unmerklicher, aber stetiger Steigerung immer lebhafter.

SYMPHONY NO. 1 IN D MAJOR SYMPHONY NO. 1 IN D MAJOR    45

# TRIO.

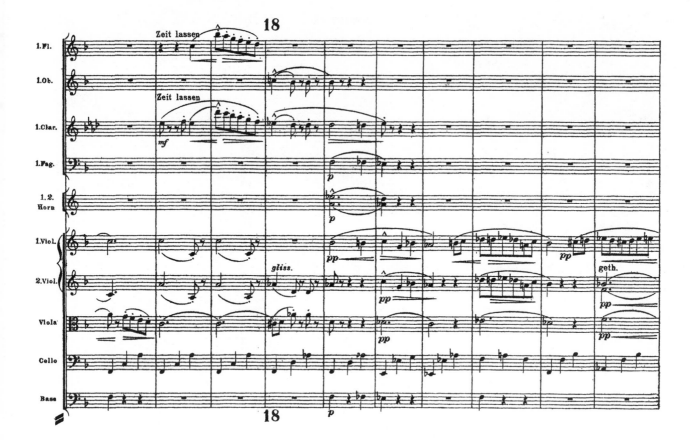

SYMPHONY NO. 1 IN D MAJOR  67

# 3

14

*) Anmerkung für den Dirigenten: Kein Irrthum! Mit dem Holz zu streichen.

# 4

1. 2. Picc.
1. 2. Fl.
1. 4. Ob. 2. 3.
1. 2. in C Clar.
3. in C Clar.
4. in Es
1. 2. 3. Fag.
1. 3. 5. Horn 2. 4. 6. 7.
1. 2. Trmp. 3. 4.
1. 2. Pos.
3. Pos. Tuba
1. Pauker 2.
Becken
Gr. Tr.
1. Viol.
2. Viol.
Viola
Cello
Bass
zu 2
zu 3
zu 4
offen
Dämpfer auf
3. Pos.
geth.

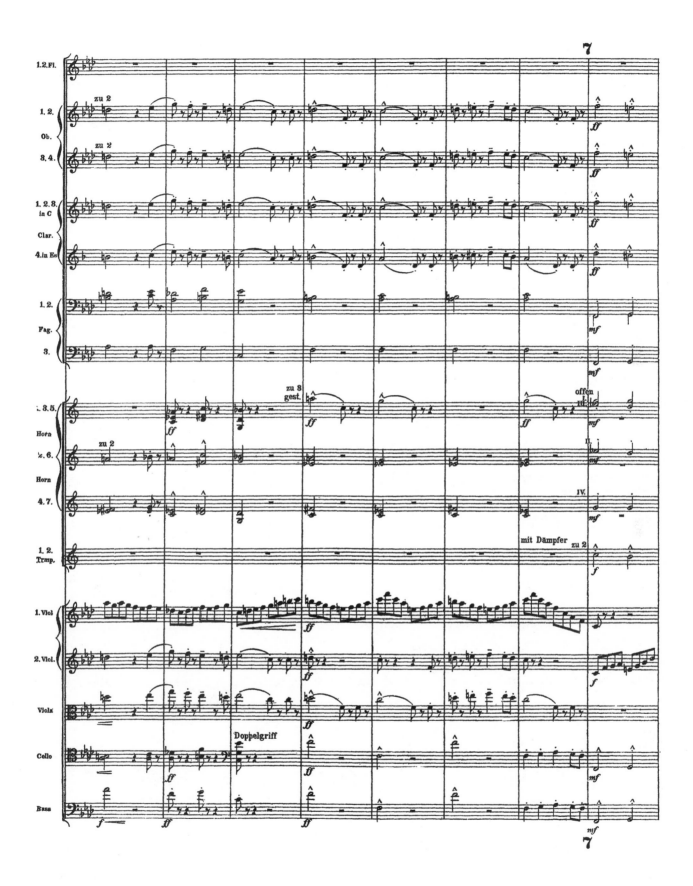

9
Zurückhalten.
zu 2
a tempo
1.2. Picc.
1.2. Fl.
1. 4. Oboe 2. 3.
1. in C Clar. 2.3. in C
Clar. 4. in Es
1. 2. Fag. 3.
1. 2. Horn
3. 4. Horn
5. 6. Horn
7.
1. 2. Trmp. 3. 4.
1. 2. Pos.
3. Pos. und Tuba
1. Pauker 2.
Gr. Tr.
geth.
1. Viol. 2.
Viola
Cello
unis.
9 Zurückhalten.
a tempo

1.2. Fl.
1.4.
Oboe
2.3.
1.
Clar. in C
2.3.
1.2.
Fag.
3.
1.2.
Horn
3.4.
Horn
5.6.
Horn
7.
1.2.
Trmp.
3.4.
1.2. Pos.
3. Pos. und Tuba
1. Pauker
Becken
Gr. Tr.
1.
Viol.
2.
Viola
Cello
Bass
zu 2
gest.
offen
fp molto cresc.
ffp molto cresc.
mit Schwammschlägel
poco cresc.
molto cresc.
cresc.

10
1.2. Picc.
zu 2
ff
1.2. Fl.
zu 2
1.4. Oboe 2.3.
1. in C. Clar.
2.3. Clar.
4. in Es
1. 2. Fag. 3.
1. 2. Horn
3.4. Horn
5. 6. Horn
7
offen
1. 2. Trmp. 3.4.
fp
1.2. Pos.
3. Pos. und Tuba
1. Pauker
Gr. Tr.
f
1. Viol. 2.
Viola
Cello
Bass
10

zu 2
1.2. Fl.
1.4.
Oboe
2.3.
I.in C
Clar.
2.3.
Clar.
4.in Es
1. 2.
Fag.
3.
1.2.
Horn
3.4.
Horn
5.6.
Horn
7.
1. 2.
Trmp.
3.4.
1.2.Pos.
3.Pos. und Tuba
1.
Pauker
2.
Gr.Tr.
1.
Viol.
2.
Viola
Cello
Bass

33
a tempo. Vorwärts.
Luftpause
molto rit.
zu 2
zu 3
1. 2. Picc.
1. 2. Fl.
1. Ob.
2. 3. Ob.
4.
1. 2. 3. in C
Clar.
4. in Es
1. 2. Fag.
3.
1. 2. Horn
3. 4. Horn
5. 6. 7.
1. 2. Trmp.
3. 4.
1. 2. Pos.
3. Pos. Tuba
1. Pauker 2.
Trgl.
1. Viol.
2. Viol.
Viola
Cello
Bass
stacc.
pesante
molto riten.
C nach D, G nach A.
Hoch G nach C
rit.
geth.
molto rit. a tempo. Vorwärts.
33
Luftpause

Anmerkung für den Dirigenten: Die Betonungen *fp* in den Violen, Celli u. Bässen sowie auch in den andern Instrumenten werden entsprechend dem allgemei-
nen **Diminuendo** immer schwächer und schwächer ausgeführt.

43.

SYMPHONY NO. 1 IN D MAJOR   151

Die Holzinstrumente Schalltr. in die Höhe.

*) Anmerkung. Von hier an (und zwar ja nicht 4 Takte vorher) bis zum Schluss ist es empfehlenswerth die Hörner so lange zu verstärken, bis der hymnenartige, alles übertönende Choral die nöthige Klangfülle erreicht hat. Alle Hornisten stehen auf, um die möglichst grösste Schallkraft zu erzielen.

59

1.2. Fl.
zu 2
.2.3.4. Ob.
zu 4
.2. in C Clar.
3. in C Clar.
4. in Es
1. Fag.
2. 3.
1.2. Horn
3.4. Horn
5.6. Horn
7.
Hörner Verstkng.
1.2. Trmp.
3.4.
1.2. Pos.
3. Pos. Tuba
1. Pauker 2.
Triangel
Becken
Gr. Tr.
1. Viol. 2.
Viola
Cello
Bass

61
1.2. Picc.
1.2. Fl.
1.4 Ob. 2.3.
1.2. in C Clar.
3. in C Clar.
4. in Es
1. Fag. 2.3.
Hörner-Verstärkung unisono mit 1. und 2. Horn
1.2. Horn
3.4. Horn
5.6. Horn
7.
1.2. Trmp.
3.4.
1.2. Pos.
3. Pos. Tuba
1. Pauker 2.
Triangel
Becken
Gr. Tr.
1. Viol. 2.
Viola
Cello
Bass
zu 2
geth.
ff
fff
61

# SYMPHONY NO. 2

# List of Instruments and Voices

4 Flutes [Flöte, Fl.], alternating on
    4 Piccolos
4 Oboes [Oboe, Ob.], two alternating on
    2 English Horns [Engl. Horn]
3 Clarinets [Clarinette, Clar.] (B♭, A, C), one alternating on
    Bass Clarinet [Bass-Clarinette, Basscl.] (B♭)
2 E♭ Clarinets, one alternating on
    Clarinet (both doubled in *ff* where possible)
3 Bassoons [Fagott, Fag.]
Contrabassoon [Contra-Fagott, Contrafg.], alternating on
    Bassoon

10 Horns [Horn] (F), four used offstage [in der Ferne]
8–10 Trumpets [Trompete, Trmp.] (F, C), four to six used offstage
4 Trombones [Posaune, Pos.]
Contrabass-Tuba [Contrabasstuba, Tuba]

7 Timpani [Pauken], six (three players) onstage, one offstage
2 pairs of Cymbals [Becken], one offstage
2 Triangles [Triangel], one offstage
Side Drum [Kleine Trommel, Kl. Tr.] (more than one, where
    possible)
Glockenspiel
3 Bells [Glocken] (steel rods with deep, unpitched sound)
2 Bass Drums [Grosse Trommel, Gr. Tr.], one offstage, with
    Switch [Ruthe]
2 Tam-tams [Tam-Tam] (high and low)

*Percussion requires total of 7 players*

Harps [Harfe] I, II (several per part)

Organ [Orgel]

Violins [Violine, Viol.] I, II
Violas [Viola]
Cellos [Violoncello, Cello]
Basses [Contrabass, Bass] (several with low C-string)

*Largest possible contingent of all strings*

Soprano solo [Sopran-Solo, Sopr. Solo]
Alto solo [Altstimme, Altst., Alt. Solo]
Sopranos [Soprane, Sopr.]
Altos [Alte, Alt.]
Tenors [Tenore, Ten.]
Basses [Bässe, Bass]

# Symphony No. 2

## 1

Allegro maestoso. Mit durchaus ernstem und feierlichem Ausdruck.

1. 2. Flöte.

3. Flöte (Piccolo) (im *ff* doppelt besetzt.)

1. 2. Oboe.

3. Oboe (engl. Horn.)

Engl. Horn.

1. 2. 3. Clarinette in B.
(3. nimmt zuweilen Bassclar. in B.)

1. 2. Clarinette in Es.

1. 2. Fagott.

zu 2

3. Fagott (Contrafagott.)

Contrafagott

6 Hörner in F.
(Die Bezeichnung „gestopft" gilt, bis sie durch
eine neue „offen" wieder aufgehoben ist.)

4 Trompeten in F.
(1. Tromp. im *ff* doppelt besetzt.)

4 Posaunen.
(mit Sordinen versehen)

Contrabasstuba.

Triangel. Tam-tam. (tief)

Becken (abwechselnd mit einem Tam-
tam, welches höher klingt als das 1. und
mit Tam-tam (hoch) bezeichnet ist.)

Grosse Trommel.

1. 2. Pauke.

1. 2. Harfe.

Allegro maestoso. Mit durchaus ernstem und feierlichem Ausdruck.

1. Violine.
trem. (nicht theilen.)

2. Violine
trem. (nicht theilen.)

Viola.
trem. (getheilt.)

Violoncell.
wild

Contrabass.
(mindestens einige davon mit Contra-C-Saite)
wild

Allegro maestoso. Mit durchaus ernstem und feierlichem Ausdruck.

Anmerkung für den Dirigenten. In den ersten Takten des Thema's sind die Bassfiguren schnell in heftigem Ansturm ungefähr ♩=144, die Pausen jedoch im Hauptzeitmass
♩=84—92 auszuführen. Der Halt im 4. Takte ist kurz — gleichsam ein Ausholen zu neuer Kraft.

*) untere Stimme nur von den mit Contra-C versehenen Bässen auszuführen.

1. Piccolo.
1.2. Fl.
1.2. Ob. 3.
1.2. in B. Clar. 1.2. in Es.
1.2. Fag.
Contrafag.
1.2. Horn in F
3. 5. Horn in F 4. 6.
1. 2. Trmp in F. 3. 4.
1. 2. Pos. 3.
4. Pos. u. Tuba.
Becken.
Gr. Tr.
1. Pauke 2.
1. Viol.
2. Viol.
Viola.
Cello.
Bass.
zu 2
Schalltrichter auf.
cresc.
D nach Es hoch.
tief E nach Es tief.
D nach Cis.

Poco rit.
1.2.Piccolo.
1.2. Fl.
1.2.3. Ob.
1.2. in B.
Clar.
1.2. in Es.
1.2. Fag.
Contrafag.
1. 2. Horn in F.
3. 4. Horn in F.
5. 6.
1. 2. Trmp. in F.
3. 4.
1. 2. Pos.
3. Pos.
4.
Tuba.
Triangel.
Becken.
1. Pauke. 2.
1.Viol. geth.
2.Viol. geth.
Violen geth
Cello u. Bass.
zu 2.
zu 3.
I.
II. III.
offen
klingen lassen
Schwammschl.
molto cresc.
dim.
Poco rit.

1.2.Piccolo.
1.2.Fl.
1.2.3.Ob.
1 2 in B. Clar.
1.2.in Es.
1.2.Fag.
Contrafag.
1.2. Horn in F.
3.4. Horn in F.
5.6.
1.2. Trmp. in F.
3.4
1.2. Pos.
3. Pos.
4.
Tuba.
Tam-tam (hoch.)
Gr. Tr.
Tam-tam. (tief.)
1. Pauke. 2.
1.u.2. Harfe.
1.Viol.
2.Viol.
Viola.
Cello.
Bass.
zu 2.
zu 3.
sempre ff
cresc.
gewöhnlich
B nach C
Es nach G hoch
B nach G
Es nach C
gestrichen
ff sempre
geth.
sempre
I.II.
III.
II.
I.

Etwas drängend.
zu 2.
1.2. Piccolo.
1.2. Fl.
1.2. Ob.
3.
1.2. in B. Clar.
1.2. in Es.
1.2. Fag.
Contrafag.
1.2. Horn in F.
3.4. Horn in F.
5.6.
mit aufgehobenem Schalltrichter.
1.2. Trmp. in F.
3.4.
1.2. Pos.
3. Pos.
4.
Tuba.
Etwas drängend.
1. Viol.
sempre ff
2. Viol.
sempre ff
Viola.
Cello.
Bass.
Etwas drängend.

1.2.Piccolo.
1.2.Fl.
1.2.
Ob.
3.
1.2. in B.
Clar.
1.2. in Es.
1.2. Fag.
Contrafag.
1. 2.
Horn in F.
3. 4.
Horn in F.
5. 6.
1. 2.
Trmp. in F.
3. 4.
1. 2.
Pos.
3. 4.
Tuba.
Becken.
1.
Pauke.
2.
1.Viol.
2.Viol.
Viola.
Cello.
Bass.
zu 2
zu 2.
gest.
gest. zu 2.
mit Schlägel
gleich abdämpfen
dito
kleine Pauke
sempre ff
nicht geth.

22
1.-2.
Fl.
3.
1. 2. Ob.
engl. Horn
1. 2. in B.
Clar.
3. in C.
1. 2. Fag.
Contrafag.
1. 2.
Horn in F.
3. 4.
Horn in F.
5. 6.
1. 2.
Trmp. in F.
3. 4.
1. 2.
Pos.
3. 4.
Tuba
1. Viol.
2. Viol.
Viola
Cello
Bass
zu 2.
22

236 SYMPHONY NO. 2 IN C MINOR

# 3

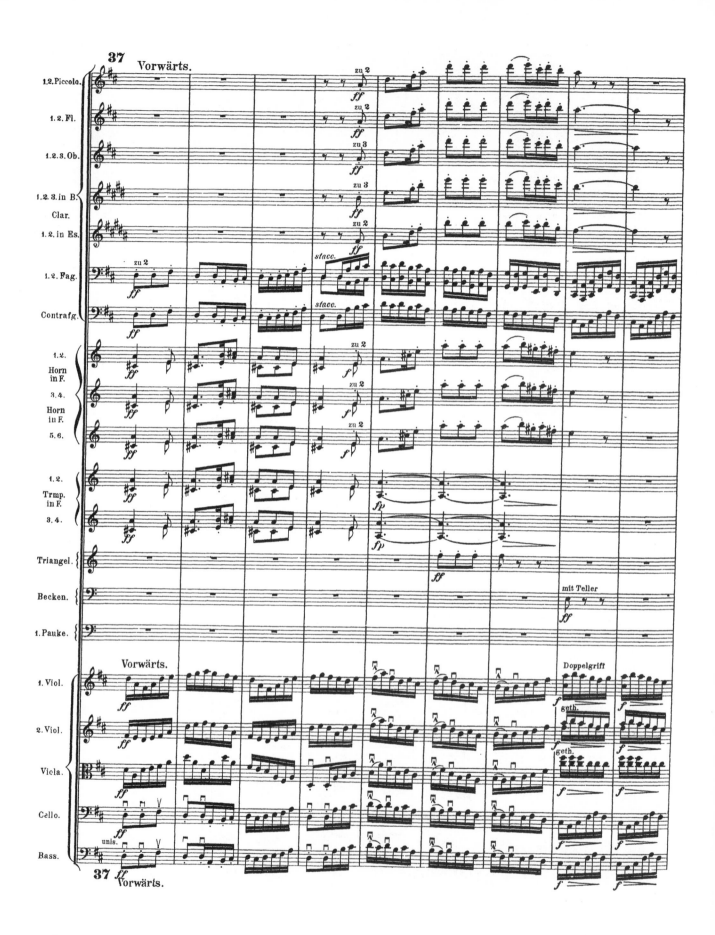

40
Sehr getragen und gesangvoll.
1.2.3. Fl.
1.2.3. Ob.
1.2.3. in C. Clar.
1.2. in Es
1.2. Fag.
Contrafg.
1.2. Horn in F. 3.4
1. Trmp. in F.
2. Trmp. in F.
3. Trmp. in F.
4.
3. Pos. u. Tuba
Triangel.
1. Pauke 2.
1 Harfe
2. Harfe
1. Viol.
2. Viol.
Viola.
Cello.
Bass.
zu 3
zu 2
(2. Es Clar. nimmt B Clar. und ist als 4. Clar. notirt.)
Schalltrichter in die Höhe.
sehr hervortretend
sehr ausdrucksvoll gesungen
E nach Es. H nach A.
mit Dämpfer
pizz.
Sehr getragen und gesangvoll.
40 Sehr getragen und gesangvoll.

1.2. Fl. 3.
1.2. Ob. 3.
zu 2.
1.Clar.
dim.
1.Clar.in Es.
2.3. in A.
zu 2.
1.2. Fag.
Contrafg.
gest.
1.2. Horn in F.
3.4. Horn in F.
5.6.
1.2. Tromp. in F. 3.4.
3. Pos. Tuba
mit Holzschlägel.
Becken
Gr.Tr.
(klingen lassen.)
Tam-tam (tief.)
arco
1. Viol. geth.
2. Viol. geth.
ohne Dämpfer
Violen geth.
dim.
gliss.
pizz.
Cello
Bass
geth.

49
Unmerklich drängend
1.2.Piccolo
1.2.Fl.
1.
Ob.
2.3.
1.2.3.in B.
Clar.
1.2.in Es.
1.2.Fag.
Contrafg.
1.3.5.
Horn
in F.
2.4.6.
5.6.Horn offen.
1.2.
Trmp.
in F.
3.4.
1.2.
Pos.
3.4.
Tuba
Tam-tam
(hoch)
Tam-tam
(tief)
Gr.Tr.
1.
Pauke
2.
1.Viol.
2.Viol.
Viola
Cello
Bass
zu 2.
zu 3.
Schalltr. auf
cresc.
(klingen lassen.)
mit Holzschlägel.
Unmerklich drängend.
geth.
arco
trem.
49
Unmerklich drängend

50
1.2.Piccolo
1.2. Fl.
1.
Ob.
2. 3.
1.2.3. in B.
Clar.
1.2. in Es.
1.2. Fag.
Contrafg.
1.3.5.
Horn
in F.
2.4.6.
1.2.
Trmp.
in F.
3.4.
1.2.
Pos.
3.4.
Tuba
Tam-tam
(hoch)
Tam-tam
(tief)
Becken
1. Viol.
2. Viol.
Viola
Cello
Bass
zu 2
zu 3
fff
ff
fp
mf
cresc.
unisono
50

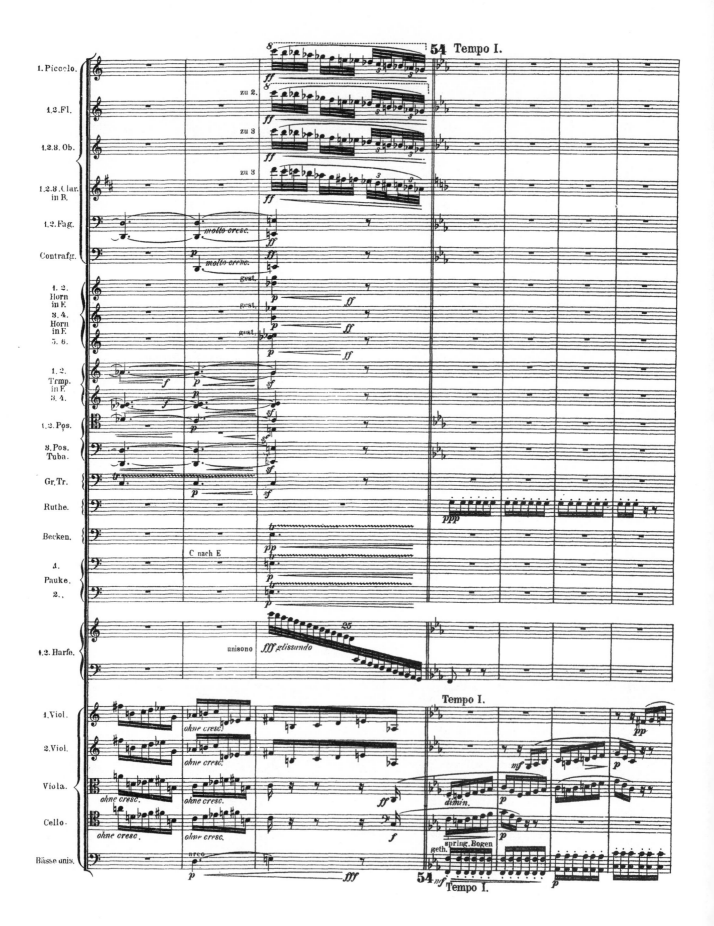

Folgt ohne jede Unterbrechung der 4. Satz.

attacca: **4**

## "URLICHT"
(from *Des Knaben Wunderhorn*)

**296**   *SYMPHONY NO. 2 IN C MINOR*

attacca: 5
Im Tempo des Scherzo's.
Wild herausfahrend.
1.2. Flöte.
(abwechselnd 3.4. Piccolo.)
3.4. Flöte.
(abwechselnd 1.2. Piccolo.)
1.2. Oboe.
3.4. Oboe.
(abwechselnd 1.2. engl. Horn.)
1.2.3. Clarinette in B.
(3. Clar. abwechselnd Bassclar. in B.)
1.2. Clarinette in Es.
(2. Es-Clar. abwechselnd 4. Clarinette.)
1.2.3. Fagott.
4. Fagott.
(abwechselnd Contrafagott.)
1.2.3.4.
Horn in F.
5.6.
1.2.3.4. Horn in F in der Ferne; sind an den in der Partitur bemerkten Stellen mit im Orch. thätig.
1.2.3.4.
Trompete in F.
5.6.
1.2.3.4. Trp. in F in der Ferne; (zwei davon können durch die 5. u. 6. Orch-Trp. ausgef. werden)
Triangel, Becken, grosse Trommel und Pauke in der Ferne.
1. 2. Posaune.
3. 4. Posaune u. Tuba.
Becken.
Grosse Trommel.
Tam-tam. (tief.)
1. Pauker.
(Jeder mit 3 Pauken.)
2. Pauker.
Glockenspiel. Kleine Trommel.
Tam-tam. (hoch.)
3 Glocken. (Stahlstäbe von tiefem unbestimmtem Klange.)
Orgel.
1. 2. Harfe. (Jede mehrfach besetzt.)
1. Violinen.
2. Violinen
Viola.
Sopr. Solo. Alt Solo.
Gemischter Chor.
Violoncello u. Contrabass.
zu 2.
1.2. Fl.
zu 2.
Picc.
3. u 4. Ob.
1.2.3. Clar.
1.2. Es Clar.
Contrafag.
mit aufgehobenem Schalltrichter
mit aufgehob. Schalltrichter
zu 2
mit aufgehob. Schalltrichter
4. Pos.
Tuba
mit aufgehob. Schalltrichter
mit Holzschlägeln.
Im Tempo des Scherzo's.
Wild herausfahrend.
ohne Dämpfer
pizz.
arco
8 fach geth.
4 fach geth.
geth.
vereint
ohne Dämpfer

Anmerkung für den Dirigenten: überall schnell abdämpfen.
(1. 2.) Fl. / 3. 4. Picc.
1. 2. Picc.
1. 2. Ob. 3. 4.
1. 2. 3. in B Clar.
1. 2. in Es.
1. 2. 3. Fag.
Contrafag.
1. 2. 7. 9. Horn in F.
3. 4. Horn in F.
5. 6. 8. 10.
1. 2. Trmp. in F.
3. 4. Trmp. in F.
5. 6.
1. 2. Pos. 3. 4.
Tuba.
Becken.
1. Pauke 2.
1. Viol.
2. Viol.
Viola.
Cello.
Bass.
nehmen grosse Flöte.
nehmen grosse Flöte.
zu 2.
zu 3.
ohne Verstärkung.
mit Tellern.
Es nach C. C nach A.
C nach D.

1.2. Fl.
1.2. Picc.
1.2. Ob.
3.4.
1.2. in B.
1.2. in Es.
1.2. Fag.
3.
Contrafag.
1.2. Horn in F.
3.4. Horn in F.
5.6.
1.2. Trmp. in F.
3.4.
1.2. Pos.
3.4.
Tuba
2. Pauke
1. Viol.
2. Viol.
Viola
Cello
Bass
zu 2.
ff
fp
molto cresc.
zu 2. Schalltr. auf
Schalltrichter auf
sempre geth.
mf
p
f

336   SYMPHONY NO. 2 IN C MINOR

19
1.2. Fl.
zu 2.
1.2.
Ob.
3.4.
zu 2.
ohne Nachschl.
zu 3.
1.2.3. in B.
Clar.
1.2. in Es.
1.2
Fag.
3.
Contrafag.
1.2.
Horn in F.
3.4.
Horn in F.
5.6.
zu 3.
1.2.5.
Trmp. in F.
3.
Trmp. in F.
4.
1.2.
Pos.
3.4.
Tuba
Triangel
Becken
C nach B
1.
Pauke
2.
1.Viol.
ff sempre
2.Viol.
Viola
Cello
Bass
19

1.2. Fl.
1.2. Picc.
1.2. Ob.
3.4.
1.2.3. in B. Clar.
1.2. in Es.
1.2. Fag.
3.
Contrafag.
1.2. Horn in F
3.4. Horn in F
5.6.
1.2. Trmp. in F
3.4. Trmp. in F
5.6.
1.2. Pos.
3.4.
Tuba
Becken
1 Pauke 2
1. Viol.
2. Viol.
Viola
Cello
Bass
zu 2.
zu 3.
Ges nach F.

**22 Mit etwas drängendem Charakter.**

Anmerkung für den Dirigenten: muss so schwach erklingen, dass es den Charakter der Gesangstelle, Celli und Fag. in keinerlei Weise tangiert. Der Autor denkt sich hier, ungefähr, vom Wind vereinzelnd herüber getragene Klänge einer kaum vernehmbaren Musik.

**22 Mit etwas drängendem Charakter.**
(NB. alle Pausen gut gehalten)

**23**

*SYMPHONY NO. 2 IN C MINOR* 343

346 SYMPHONY NO. 2 IN C MINOR

Immer noch drängend.
1.2. Fl.
1.2. Picc.
1.2. Ob. 3.4.
1.2.3. in B. Clar. 1.2 in Es
1.2. Fag. 3.
Contrafag.
1.2. Horn in F.
3.4. Horn in F.
5.6.
1.2. Trmp. in F.
3.4. Trmp. in F.
5.6.
1.2. Pos. 3.4.
Tuba.
1.Viol.
2.Viol.
Viola.
Cello.
Bass.
zu 2.
zu 3
gest.
offen
nicht theilen
f espress.
sempre cresc.
Immer noch drängend.
Immer noch drängend.

26
Più mosso.
accel.
1.2. Fl.
1.2. Picc.
1. 2. Ob. 3. 4.
1.2.3. in B. Clar. 1.2. in Es.
1. 2. Fag. 3.
Contrafag.
1. 2. Horn in F. 3. 4. Horn in F. 5. 6.
1. 2. Trmp. in F. 3. 4. Trmp. in F. 5. 6.
1. 2. Pos. 3. 4.
Tuba.
Triangel.
Gr. Trom.
Becken.
Tam-tam. (tief.)
1. Pauke 2.
1. Viol.
2. Viol.
Viola.
Cello.
Bass.
zu 2
zu 3
Zungenstoss
Zungenst.
mit aufgehobenem Schalltrichter.
gestopft
offen
cresc.
sehr kurz
sempre cresc.
molto cresc.
mit Paukenschlägeln
klingen lassen
O nach Des
sempre ff

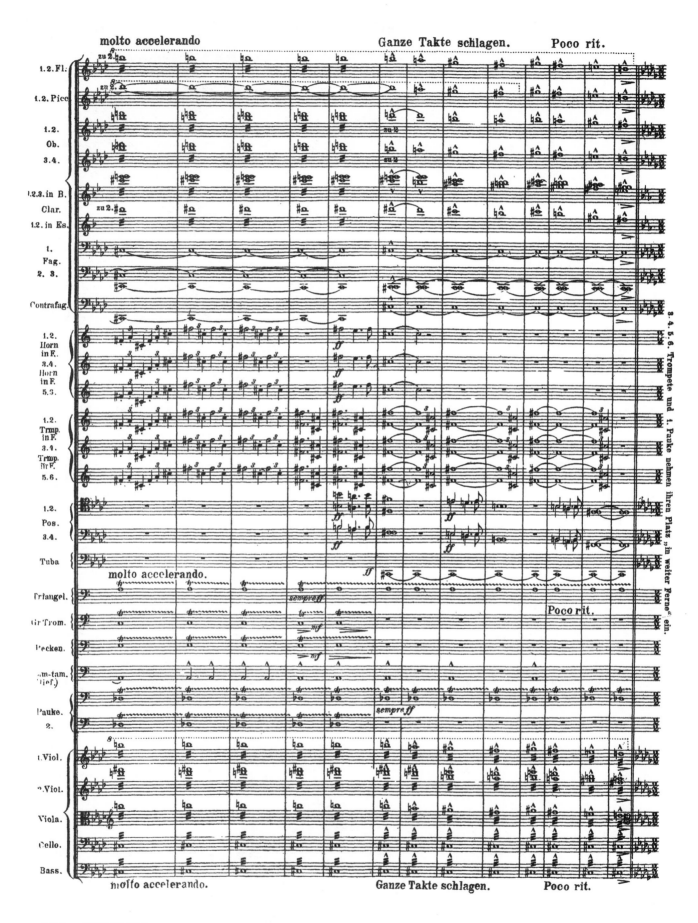

Anmerkung für den Dirigenten: die 4 Trompeten müssen aus entgegengesetzter Richtung her erklingen.

Zur Vereinfachung des orchestralen Apparates ist darauf Rücksicht genommen, dass diese Trompeten, falls es nöthig ist, von den im Orchester wirkenden Musikern (3.4.5.6. Trompete) ausgeführt werden können, und haben dieselben Zeit genug ihre Plätze zu wechseln.

(Anmerkung: Die Striche | bedeuten die Stelle, wo die verschiedenen Instrumente im Rhythmus zusammenfallen sollen.)

**31  Langsam. Misterioso.**

Sopr. Solo (ohne im Geringsten hervorzutreten.)

Auf-er-steh'n, ja auf-er-steh'n wirst du, mein Staub, nach kur-zer Ruh!

Auf-er-steh'n, ja auf-er-steh'n wirst du, mein Staub, nach kur-zer Ruh!

Auf-er-steh'n, ja auf-er-steh'n wirst du, mein Staub, nach kur-zer Ruh!

Auf-er-steh'n, ja auf-er-steh'n wirst du, mein Staub, nach kur-zer Ruh!

Auf-er-steh'n, ja auf-er-steh'n wirst du, mein Staub, nach kur-zer Ruh!

\*) Anmerkung für das Studium: Die 2. Bässe nicht eine Octave höher, sonst würde die vom Autor intendirte Wirkung ausbleiben; es kommt durchaus nicht darauf an, diese tiefen Töne zu hören, sondern durch diese Schreibart sollen nur die tiefen Bässe verhindert werden, etwa das obere B zu „nehmen," und so die obere Note zu verstärken.

32
Sehr zart
hervortr.
innig
Sopr. Solo.
Sopr.
Alt.
Ten.
Bass.
Un - sterb-lich Le - ben! Un - ster - lich Le - ben wird der dich rief, dich rief
1. 2. 3. Pos.
1. Viol.
Viola.
Cello u. Bass.
NB. mit Dämpfer
mit Dämpfer
mit Dämpfer
NB. An dieser Stelle wirken die Posaunen, Violinen und Viol. nur im Notfalle mit, wenn es gilt den Chor vor „Fallen" zu bewahren.
33 Sehr breit.
1. 2. Horn in F.
3. 4. Horn in F.
5. 6.
zu 2
1. Trmp. in F.
2. Trmp. in F.
3.
p molto portamento
2. Pauker.
Alle Harfen.
Sehr breit.
1. Viol. 4 fach geth.
2. Viol.
ohne Dämpfer
geth.
sempre ppp
gänzlich verschwindend
Sopr. Solo
dir ge - - - - ben
Cello u. Bass.
33
sempre ppp

Anmerkung für den Dirigenten: Die früher in der Ferne aufgestellten 4 Hörner mögen zur Verstärkung dieses Thema's herangezogen werden, ebenso in allen darauf folgenden eigens bezeichneten Stellen.

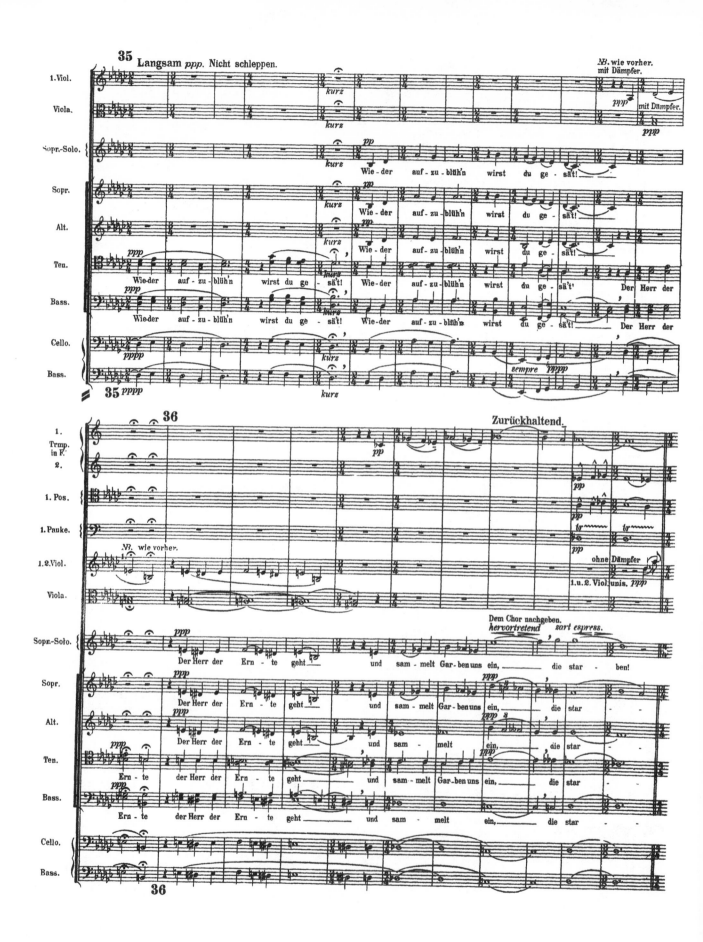

49 Wieder zurückhaltend.
Rit.
alle 4 mit Piccolo.
1.2.3 4.Picc.
1 2. Ob. 3.4.
1.2.3.in B. Clar.
1.2. in Es.
1. 2. Fag. 3.
Contrafag.
1.3.5.7.9. Horn in F 2.4.6.8.10.
mit aufgehobenen Schalltrichter.
1. 2. Trmp. in F. 3. 4. Trmp. in F. 5. 6
1 2 3. Pos.
4. Tuba.
Triangel.
Becken. Gr.Tr.
2. Pauke.
Des nach As. F nach Es.(tief.)
Orgel.
1.Viol.
2.Viol.
Viola.
Sopr.
Alt.
Ten.
Bass.
Cello & Bass.
Portamento
molto cresc.
unis.
schla - gen, was du ge- schla - gen, zu Gott, zu Gott, zu Gott wird es dich

# Texts and Translations

URLICHT
O Röschen roth!
Der Mensch liegt in größter Noth!
Der Mensch liegt in größter Pein!
Je lieber möcht' ich in Himmel sein!
Da kam ich auf einen breiten Weg;
Da kam ein Engelein und wollt' mich abweisen.
Ach nein! Ich ließ mich nicht abweisen:
Ich bin von Gott und will wieder zu Gott!
Der liebe Gott wird mir ein Lichtchen geben,
Wird leuchten mir bis in das ewig selig Leben!

      —DES KNABEN WUNDERHORN

PRIMAL LIGHT
O little red rose!
Man lies in the greatest need.
Man lies in the greatest suffering.
How much rather would I be in Heaven!
I came upon a broad road.
There came an angel and wanted to block my way.
Ah no! I did not let myself be turned away!
I am of God, and to God I shall return.
Dear God will grant me a small light,
Will light my way to eternal, blissful life.

      —DES KNABEN WUNDERHORN


AUFERSTEH'N
Aufersteh'n, ja aufersteh'n wirst du,
Mein Staub, nach kurzer Ruh!
Unsterblich Leben
Wird der dich rief dir geben.

Wieder aufzublüh'n wirst du gesät!
Der Herr der Ernte geht
Und sammelt Garben
Uns ein, die starben.

      —FRIEDRICH KLOPSTOCK

RESURRECTION
Arise, yes, you will arise from the dead,
My dust, after a short rest!
Eternal life
Will be given you by Him who called you.

To bloom again are you sown.
The lord of the harvest goes
And gathers the sheaves,
Us who have died.

      —FRIEDRICH KLOPSTOCK


O glaube, mein Herz, o glaube:
Es geht dir nichts verloren!

Dein ist, was du gesehnt!
Dein, was du geliebt, was du gestritten!

O glaube:
Du wardst nicht umsonst geboren!
Hast nicht umsonst gelebt, gelitten!

Was entstanden ist, das muß vergehen!
Was vergangen, auferstehen!
Hör' auf zu beben!
Bereite dich zu leben!

Oh believe, my heart, oh believe,
Nothing will be lost to you!

Everything is yours that you have desired,
Yours, what you have loved, what you have struggled for.

Oh believe,
You were not born in vain,
Have not lived in vain, suffered in vain!

What was created must perish.
What has perished must rise again.
Tremble no more!
Prepare yourself to live!

O Schmerz! Du Alldurchdringer!
Dir bin ich entrungen!
O Tod! Du Allbezwinger!
Nun bist du bezwungen!
Mit Flügeln, die ich mir errungen
In heißem Liebesstreben
Werd' ich entschweben
Zum Licht, zu dem kein Aug' gedrungen!
Sterben werd' ich, um zu leben!

Aufersteh'n, ja aufersteh'n wirst du,
Mein Herz, in einem Nu!
Was du geschlagen,
Zu Gott wird es dich tragen!

        —*GUSTAV MAHLER*

O Sorrow, all-penetrating!
I have been wrested away from you!
O Death, all-conquering!
Now you are conquered!
With wings that I won
In the passionate strivings of love
I shall mount
To the light to which no sight has penetrated.
I shall die, so as to live!

Arise, yes, you will arise from the dead,
My heart, in an instant!
What you have conquered*
Will bear you to God.

        —*GUSTAV MAHLER*

*Or, "Your [heart]beats," i.e., what you have lived through.